WRESTLING SUPERSTARS

THE UNDERTAKER

By J. R. Kinley

Kaleidoscope
Minneapolis, MN

BIGFOOT BOOKS

The Quest for Discovery Never Ends

This edition first published in 2020 by Kaleidoscope Publishing, Inc.

For information regarding permission, write to Kaleidoscope Publishing, Inc.
6012 Blue Circle Drive
Minnetonka, MN 55343

Library of Congress Control Number
2019940207

ISBN
978-1-64519-090-5 (library bound)
978-1-64494-229-1 (paperback)
978-1-64519-193-3 (ebook)

Printed in the United States of America.

Bigfoot lurks within one of the images in this book. It's up to you to find him!

TABLE OF
CONTENTS

Chapter 1: **The Deadman** *4*

Chapter 2: **This Is the Undertaker** *10*

Chapter 3: **Telling a Story** *16*

Chapter 4: **The Streak** *22*

Beyond the Book *28*

Research Ninja *29*

Further Resources *30*

Glossary *31*

Index *32*

Photo Credits *32*

About the Author *32*

The Deadman

People called the Undertaker the Deadman. He lost a match with Yokozuna. Yokozuna locked him in a casket. He rolled the Undertaker away. A bell rang. Then the arena went dark. The Undertaker appeared on a screen. He said he would be reborn. He would not rest in peace. He was gone for many months.

Ted DiBiase was a World Wrestling Federation (WWF) wrestler. He said he found the Undertaker. He brought him back to WWF. But the Undertaker's manager came forward. His name was Paul Bearer. Bearer said the real Undertaker was with him. He said DiBiase's Undertaker was an **impostor**. Which was the real Undertaker?

The Undertaker is a wrestling legend.

Fans would find out at SummerSlam 1994. The match was called "Undertaker vs. Undertaker." The real Undertaker would win. That would solve the mystery.

DiBiase and his Undertaker stood in the ring. Bearer walked in. Two men in black hoods brought a casket. Scary organ music played. White smoke came out of the casket. Bearer lifted an **urn** from it. This urn supposedly held the Undertaker's power. He lifted the lid. It glowed from inside. Then a bell rang. A figure appeared. He wore a long black coat. A wide-brimmed hat cast shadows on his face. The fans went wild.

Caskets are used to bury the dead. The Undertaker would sometimes push his opponents into caskets.

The two wrestlers faced each other. Their long hair hid their faces. Bearer's Undertaker wore purple gloves and boots. DiBiase's wore gray ones. The gray Undertaker threw a punch. But the purple Undertaker stopped it. He kicked and punched his opponent. They battled it out. The announcers didn't know which was the real Undertaker. The purple Undertaker climbed to the top rope. He walked the rope to the middle. Then he leapt at his opponent. An announcer said only one Undertaker could walk the ropes like that. The wrestler in purple was the real Undertaker!

The Undertaker took hard hits. But it seemed like nothing hurt him. He wrapped his arms around the impostor. He lifted him upside down. Then he slammed him into the mat. This was his Tombstone **Piledriver**. He did it again and again. Then he pinned the impostor. The real Undertaker had proven himself.

The black-hooded men returned with the casket. The Undertaker rolled the impostor inside. The true Undertaker had returned.

FUN FACT
The Undertaker is almost 7 feet (2.1 m) tall. He is one of the tallest pro wrestlers.

The Undertaker prepares for his Tombstone Piledriver.

Many fans love the Undertaker's look.

This Is the Undertaker

The Undertaker's real name is Mark Calaway. Calaway is from Texas. He played basketball in school. He could have played pro basketball in Europe. But he knew he wanted to be a wrestler.

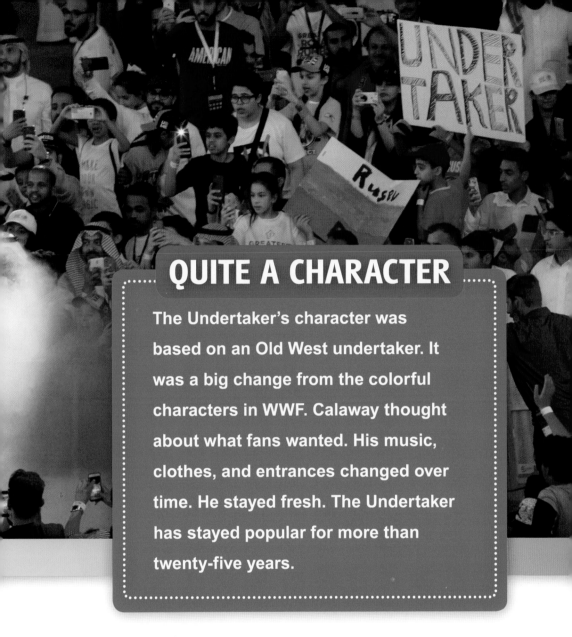

QUITE A CHARACTER

The Undertaker's character was based on an Old West undertaker. It was a big change from the colorful characters in WWF. Calaway thought about what fans wanted. His music, clothes, and entrances changed over time. He stayed fresh. The Undertaker has stayed popular for more than twenty-five years.

Calaway wrestled in different **promotions**. He wrestled for one year at World Championship Wrestling (WCW). He used the name Mean Mark Callous. WCW organizers told him that he was a good athlete. But they said no one would pay money to watch him wrestle. So he left WCW.

He met with Vince McMahon. McMahon ran WWF. Then one day, Calaway got a phone call. The person asked, "Is this the Undertaker?" Calaway wasn't sure what to say. But he realized it was McMahon. He answered, "This is the Undertaker."

FUN FACT

Calaway previously wrestled as Texas Red, the Punisher, and the Master of Pain.

The Undertaker made his WWF start at Survivor Series 1990. His team captain introduced him. He said he was from Death Valley. The Undertaker wore his **signature** black coat and hat.

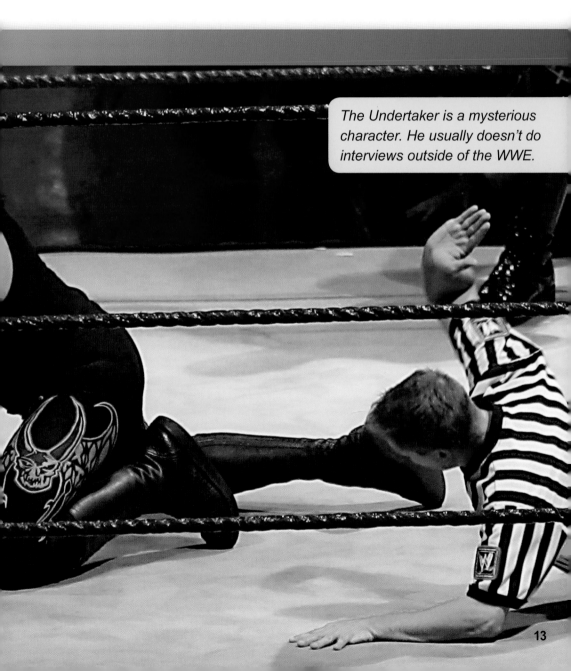

The Undertaker is a mysterious character. He usually doesn't do interviews outside of the WWE.

The Undertaker will sometimes grab people by their necks.

The next year, the Undertaker had a chance for a title. He was set to wrestle Hulk Hogan. Hogan was the WWF Champion. Fans loved him. The Undertaker waited quietly in the ring. Hogan entered to loud music. He flipped over the Undertaker's casket. The crowd chanted for Hogan. The two wrestlers threw punches. They slammed each other. Hogan hit **clotheslines**. Then the Undertaker squeezed his fingers around Hogan's head. It was a **claw hold**. But Hogan escaped.

The match was in its final moments. The Undertaker lifted Hogan upside down. He slammed him down to the mat. It was his Tombstone Piledriver. He covered him for the three-count. He won! The Undertaker took the title belt. He didn't celebrate. He carried the belt at his side. He slowly exited the arena. It was the first big victory of his career.

CHAPTER 3

Telling a Story

Wrestling is dangerous. WWE doesn't let wrestlers do some moves. Piledrivers are against the rules. But the Undertaker can still do his Tombstone Piledriver. WWE allows it because of the Undertaker's height and ability. He has had professional training. The moves are still risky, though.

It was 2007. The Undertaker was at WrestleMania 23. He was up against Batista. Batista was the WWE World Heavyweight Champion. The Undertaker had a winning streak. He had won many matches at WrestleMania. Now he wanted his first World Heavyweight Championship.

There were more than 80,000 fans in the crowd. The bell rang. Batista dove at the Undertaker. He slammed him down. But the Undertaker had the fans on his side. They cheered when he hit Batista.

Batista

The Undertaker made a fiery entrance when he faced Batista.

The Undertaker threw Batista into the corner. Then he scooped him up over his shoulder. He dropped Batista face-first onto the ring post. This was the Undertaker's Snake Eyes move. He followed it up with a boot to the chin. It sent Batista to the mat.

Next, the Undertaker climbed the ropes. He walked the top rope to the center. He jumped and clotheslined Batista. This move was called Old School.

The WWE mat is padded to help protect wrestlers from hard falls.

The Undertaker tried another move. It was called the Chokeslam. He slapped his hand onto Batista's neck. He would normally push the opponent to the mat. But Batista was strong. He pulled at the Undertaker's hand. He escaped. Later, Batista picked up the Undertaker. He slammed him down. He covered him. The announcer thought the Undertaker's winning streak was over. But the Undertaker kicked out before the three-count. The fight went on.

The Undertaker lifted Batista upside down. He dropped him to the mat. Tombstone Piledriver! He covered Batista for the three-count. The Undertaker won the title. His streak was still alive. The fans roared.

FUN FACT
The Undertaker can roll his eyes back so far that only the whites of his eyes show.

TOMBSTONE
PILEDRIVER

Flips opponent upside down

Slams opponent's head on the mat

Holds on tightly to opponent's back

CHAPTER 4

The Streak

The Undertaker has had a long career. He has wrestled for WWE for more than twenty-five years. The Undertaker is known for the Streak. This is his WrestleMania winning streak. He won twenty-one straight victories.

The Undertaker, right, has been on posters for WrestleMania.

ROMAN REIGNS®   SHANE McMAHON®

The Undertaker faced Triple H at WrestleMania in 2012. Triple H was one of his **rivals**. They stared each other down. A steel cage lowered over them.

They attacked with punches. It was a long, hard fight. The Undertaker used his Tombstone Piledriver. He covered Triple H for the three-count. The Undertaker's bell rang.

Triple H and the Undertaker traded punches as they faced each other.

After the match, he and the ref grabbed the defeated Triple H. They helped him walk out. The wrestlers' respect for each other showed. The Undertaker said, "It doesn't get much better than that."

FUN FACT

The Undertaker likes to fish. His fondest memories from childhood are fishing with his dad.

CAREER HIGHLIGHTS

1989

1989
The Undertaker joins World Championship Wrestling (WCW).

1990
The Undertaker debuts with WWF, which later becomes WWE.

1990

1991
The Undertaker begins "the Streak" at WrestleMania.

1991

1991
The Undertaker wins his first WWE Championship. The Undertaker will go on to win it three more times.

1998
The Undertaker wins his first of six Tag Team Championships, this time with partner Stone Cold Steve Austin. The Undertaker will go on to team up with the Big Show, the Rock, and Kane.

1998

2007
The Undertaker wins his first World Heavyweight Championship. He'll go on to win it two more times.

2007

2007
The Undertaker wins Royal Rumble.

The Undertaker has won seven WWE World Championships. And he's won six WWE Tag Team Championships. He still appears at WWE events. Sometimes he wrestles. WWE says his "final resting place" could be the WWE Hall of Fame. In 2019, he was not there yet. But the Undertaker is still a WWE legend.

The Undertaker has lots of fans.

THE BOOK

After reading the book, it's time to think about what you learned.
Try the following exercises to jumpstart your ideas.

THINK

DIFFERENT SOURCES. Think about the different kinds of sources
you might be able to find on the Undertaker's SummerSlam 1994 match
against the Undertaker impostor. How could each type of source be
useful in its own way?

CREATE

PRIMARY SOURCES. Primary sources are original, firsthand
resources about a person or event. Primary sources can include
interviews, videos, or photos. Create a list of the kinds of primary
sources that you might be able to find on the Undertaker.

SHARE

SUM IT UP. Write one paragraph that summarizes the important
points from the book. Remember to write your summary in your own
words—don't just copy from the book. Then, share your paragraph with a
classmate. Does your classmate have any feedback on your summary or
additional questions about the Undertaker?

GROW

REAL-LIFE RESEARCH. What places could you visit to learn more
about the Undertaker? What other things could you learn while you
were there?

RESEARCH NINJA

Visit *www.ninjaresearcher.com/0905* to learn how
to take your research skills and book report writing to the next level!

RESEARCH

DIGITAL LITERACY TOOLS

SEARCH LIKE A PRO
Learn about how to use search engines to find useful websites.

FACT OR FAKE?
Discover how you can tell a trusted website from an untrustworthy resource.

TEXT DETECTIVE
Explore how to zero in on the information you need most.

SHOW YOUR WORK
Research responsibly— learn how to cite sources.

WRITE

GET TO THE POINT
Learn how to express your main ideas.

PLAN OF ATTACK
Learn prewriting exercises and create an outline.

DOWNLOADABLE REPORT FORMS

Further Resources

BOOKS

McClellan, Ray. *Undertaker*. Bellwether Media, 2015.

O'Shei, Tim. *Undertaker*. Capstone, 2010.

Scheff, Matt. *Undertaker*. Abdo Publishing, 2014.

WEBSITES

Factsurfer.com gives you a safe, fun way to find more information.

1. Go to www.factsurfer.com.

2. Enter "The Undertaker" into the search box and click 🔍.

3. Select your book cover to see a list of related websites.

Glossary

claw hold: In a claw hold, a wrestler grips and pressures the opponent's head using all five fingers. The Undertaker held Hulk Hogan's head to the mat with a claw hold.

clotheslines: To perform clotheslines, a wrestler hits the opponent in the neck or chest with an extended arm, knocking the opponent down. Hogan hit the Undertaker with clotheslines.

impostor: An impostor is a person who pretends to be someone else. One of the Undertakers in the SummerSlam 1994 match was an impostor.

piledriver: A piledriver is an especially dangerous pro wrestling move in which a wrestler grabs his opponent, turns him upside down, and drives him headfirst into the mat. The Undertaker uses the Tombstone Piledriver as a finishing move.

promotions: Promotions are professional wrestling companies that plan and put on wrestling events. The Undertaker wrestled in different promotions.

rivals: Rivals are equally matched opponents or enemies. The Undertaker had many rivals.

signature: A signature is something that sets people apart from others. The Undertaker had a signature outfit.

urn: An urn is a vase or rounded container with a lid that holds something, often the ashes of a deceased person. The Undertaker's manager carried an urn that was believed to hold special powers.

Index

Batista, 16, 18, 20

Bearer, Paul, 4, 7–8

casket, 4, 7–8, 15

claw hold, 15

clothesline, 15, 18

DiBiase, Ted, 4, 7–8

Hogan, Hulk, 15

impostor, 4, 8

McMahon, Vince, 12

rivals, 23

SummerSlam, 7

Survivor Series, 13

Tombstone
Piledriver, 8, 15,
16, 20–21, 24

Triple H, 23–25

urn, 7

WrestleMania, 16,
22–23, 26

WWE Hall of Fame,
27

Yokozuna, 4

PHOTO CREDITS

ABOUT THE AUTHOR

J. R. Kinley is a writer and artist. She is part of a wrestling family from Ohio in one of the top wrestling regions in the nation. Her husband, Shaun Kinley, former NCAA wrestler at The Ohio State University, coaches at the nationally ranked St. Edward High School. Together, they operate Kinley Studio.